BiRD PALS

PAT JACOBS

Crabtree Publishing Company

www.crabtreebooks.com

Crabtree Publishing Company
www.crabtreebooks.com
1-800-387-7650

Published in Canada
Crabtree Publishing
616 Welland Avenue
St. Catharines, ON
L2M 5V6

Published in the United States
Crabtree Publishing
PMB 59051
350 Fifth Ave, 59th Floor
New York, NY 10118

Published in 2019 by CRABTREE PUBLISHING COMPANY.

First published in 2019 by Wayland
Copyright © Hodder and Stoughton, 2019

Author: Pat Jacobs

Editors: Victoria Brooke, Petrice Custance

Project coordinator: Kathy Middleton

Cover and interior design: Dynamo

Proofreader: Melissa Boyce

Prepress technician: Samara Parent

Print and production coordinator: Katherine Berti

Photographs:
Shutterstock: p. 10–11 (bottom)
All other images courtesy of Gettyimages iStock

Printed in the U.S.A./012019/CG20181123

Library and Archives Canada Cataloguing in Publication

Jacobs, Pat, author
        Bird pals / Pat Jacobs.

(Pet pals)
Includes index.
Issued in print and electronic formats.
ISBN 978-0-7787-5500-5 (hardcover).--
ISBN 978-0-7787-5731-3 (softcover).--
ISBN 978-1-4271-2228-5 (HTML)

        1. Cage birds--Juvenile literature. 2. Cage birds--
Behavior--Juvenile literature. I. Title.

SF461.35.J33 2018   j639.6'8   C2018-905534-0
                                              C2018-905535-9

Library of Congress Cataloging-in-Publication Data

Names: Jacobs, Pat, author.
Title: Bird pals / Pat Jacobs.
Description: New York, New York : Crabtree Publishing, 2019. |
    Series: Pet pals | Includes index.
Identifiers: LCCN 2018049839 (print) | LCCN 2018050490 (ebook) |
    ISBN 9781427122285 (Electronic) |
    ISBN 9780778755005 (hardcover : alk. paper) |
    ISBN 9780778757313 (paperback : alk. paper)
Subjects: LCSH: Cage birds--Juvenile literature. |
    Pets--Juvenile literature.
Classification: LCC SF461.35 (ebook) |
    LCC SF461.35 .J33 2019 (print) | DDC 636.6/8--dc23
LC record available at https://lccn.loc.gov/2018049839

CONTENTS

YOUR BIRD
FROM BEAK TO TAIL

Scientists believe birds **evolved** from small, meat-eating dinosaurs called theropods. Recently found **fossils** show that some of these creatures from the **Cretaceous** period had feathers. So, by getting a bird pal, you're bringing a **descendant** of a dinosaur into your home!

Wings: As a bird's wings move down, the flight feathers overlap, push against the air, and lift the bird. As the wings move up, the feathers spread out, letting air pass through.

Cere: The fleshy area above the beak is where the bird's nostrils are located, similar to a human nose.

Ears: Birds have funnel-shaped ears covered with soft feathers.

Eyes: Sight is a bird's most important sense. Birds with eyes on the sides of their head can also see behind them.

Beak: Birds don't have teeth. They pick up food with their beak and then grind it up in a special part of their stomach, called a gizzard (see page 17).

Bones: Birds have **hollow** bones. If they had solid bones, they would be too heavy to fly.

Brain: Although birds have small brains, studies suggest they are clever. In some tests, a parrot did better than a three-year-old child.

Feathers: Birds are the only animals with feathers. They are used for warmth, flight, and display. Some are brightly colored or have a special shape.

Feet: Perching birds have four toes—three facing forward and one facing back.

Tail: Tail feathers are lighter and stiffer than body feathers. Birds use their tails to take off, land, and steer during flight. Some fan their tails for display.

BIRD FACTS

- Birds have **ultraviolet (UV)** vision and many birds have markings that **reflect** UV light, which humans cannot see. For example, male and female birds called blue tits look the same to humans, but birds can tell them apart because the feathers on a male blue tit's head reflect UV light.

- There are more than 9,000 **species** of birds found throughout the world, from the frozen shores of Antarctica to tropical rain forests.

BEST BIRDS FOR BEGINNERS

Birds are intelligent and lovable pets, but they can also be demanding. It's important to choose the right feathered friend for your family. Most birds need hours of attention every day, otherwise they may get bored and start destroying furniture or household items, screeching, or plucking out their feathers.

Finches are fast fliers that need plenty of space to exercise. Happiest in small groups twittering to each other all day long, they are great fun to watch.

Budgerigars (also called parakeets or budgies) are friendly and intelligent. Spend several hours a day with them if you want them to talk. They are happiest in mixed pairs or small groups.

Canaries are perfect if you don't have much space or time. They like to live alone and are bred for their color, shape, and beautiful song. Males are the best songbirds.

Doves are quiet, gentle, and easy to **tame**. They need large cages, with UV lighting if indoors, and plenty of time to fly free. They enjoy being with their owners and other doves.

Parrotlets are little parrots with big personalities and a powerful bite! They are active, loving, and demanding, so spend plenty of time with them or they may get aggressive.

Cockatiels are playful pets and you can develop a close bond with them. These intelligent, sociable birds get depressed if left alone, so it's best to get a pair.

Lovebirds are affectionate, curious, and sometimes aggressive. It takes patience to tame them and they are noisy birds! One male or a mixed-sex pair make the best pets.

Conures are clever and relaxed. Maroon-bellied, green-cheeked, peach-fronted and dusky-headed conures are the least noisy types.

COCKATOOS AND LARGE PARROTS

You may be tempted to get a cockatoo or a large parrot, such as a macaw, but it is not recommended. These birds can live for 60 to 90 years and need a lot of care and space. If unhappy, they may pluck out their feathers, destroy everything in reach, injure people, and screech uncontrollably.

FIND YOUR PERFECT PET

When choosing your bird buddy, the first thing to decide is whether you want a beautiful songbird, a calm and gentle companion, or an active and playful pet. Do you have a lot of spare time to spend with your bird, and space for a large cage?

Feel like a chat?

NOISE LEVEL

Canaries, finches, or doves may be the best pets if you or your neighbors don't like noise. Larger parrots screech and shriek, and even budgies and cockatiels can be noisy at times.

TALKING BIRDS

There's no guarantee a bird will talk, but those in the parrot family, such as lovebirds, cockatiels, budgies, parrotlets, and conures often do. Males are more likely to talk than females. Some male budgies are real chatterboxes, with vocabularies of more than 1,000 words!

BIRDS FOR BUSY PEOPLE

Some birds need a lot of company so they don't get bored or depressed. Others can entertain themselves for most of the day, especially when they have toys and cage mates. If you're out most of the day, choose canaries, finches, budgies, or doves.

MESSY PETS

All birds throw food around but some are messier than others. Lorikeets need a special diet which makes their droppings quite messy. Cockatiels and doves create a powdery dust when they **preen**, which can cause allergic reactions in some people.

HOW LONG WILL YOUR PAL LIVE?

Many birds live for many years:

- Canaries and finches: up to 15 years
- Budgerigars: up to 18 years
- Parrotlets and lovebirds: up to 20 years
- Doves: up to 25 years
- Cockatiels: up to 30 years
- Conures: up to 35 years

GETTING PREPARED

Before you bring your new bird pal home, make sure you have everything ready so it can get settled right away.

CHOOSE A SPOT

Your bird's cage should be in a busy part of your home so it has plenty of company—but never in the kitchen. Fumes from cooking and even cleaning products can be deadly for birds. Your bird will feel safest if its cage is against a wall where it has a good view of the room but won't be startled by everyone's comings and goings. It should be protected from harsh sunlight and cool air.

EATING AND DRINKING

Food and water feeders that fit on the side of the cage are a good choice for smaller birds, and they also cut down on mess and waste. Bowls that attach to the side of the cage are better for parrots, as these mischievous birds have been known to throw bowls around, spilling their food and water. Remember to stock up on food for your pet, too. It's best to stick to the diet your bird is used to at first—and don't forget to get some treats!

FURNISH YOUR PET'S NEW HOME

Perches give your bird a place to sit and **roost**. A perch that's the wrong size can harm a bird's feet. Their nails should reach just over halfway around it. Natural wood perches are essential, while softer rope perches of different sizes will help to exercise your bird's feet.

TOYS

Birds like to keep busy, so playing is good exercise when they can't fly around. Toys help to prevent boredom and birds love to peck and chew, which keeps their beaks in good condition. They will get tired of the same toys so change them frequently.

WELCOME HOME!

Bring your bird home at a quiet time when it can settle in peacefully. Transport your new pet in a secure box with air holes and a towel in the bottom to stop your pet from sliding around. Cover the box with a cloth to make it dark and calming for your bird. Don't put your pet in the trunk of a car because exhaust fumes can be deadly.

SETTLING IN

Put your bird straight into its cage and let it get used to its new home for a couple of weeks before you try to handle it. Meanwhile, chat gently to your pet, quietly change the cage liner, and top up the food and water so it can slowly get to know you.

SET A ROUTINE

You will probably want to spoil your new feathered friend at first, but birds have good memories. They won't understand if they suddenly get less attention and fewer treats after the first few days in their new home. So set up a routine for playtime and treats that your bird pal can get used to. This is the time when you need to build a special bond with your new pet.

Make sure perches aren't positioned above food or water dishes. You don't want your pet to make a mess in its food!

BIRD-PROOF YOUR HOME

While your new bird pal is settling into its new cage, you can use the time to bird-proof the room. Birds explore with their beaks and will peck at anything, so now is the time to remove, cover, or secure any hazards, including electrical cables, aquariums, breakable objects, household chemicals, and other pets!

PET TALK

I'm really good at finding ways to escape, so please make sure my cage door has a lock.

SAFETY FIRST

Never leave a loose bird unattended, especially with a small child or another pet. Birds should not be let out in kitchens or bathrooms because there are too many things there that could harm them. Before you let your bird out of its cage, make sure there is no way it can escape from your home. Put a note on the door to let other family members know your bird is loose. Turn off ceiling fans and cover windows and mirrors or your bird may try to fly through them.

BIRD BEHAVIOR

Although your pet's life might be quite different from that of a wild bird, it will still have the same **instincts**. Understanding how wild birds behave will help you to know if your pet is acting oddly or just being a normal bird.

PREENING

Feathers are vital to a bird's survival so they spend hours preening them with their beak. As well as removing dust and **parasites**, preening spreads oil through the feathers and breaks up the **downy** ones next to the skin to create dust. This mix of oil and dust waterproofs the bird's feathers. Sometimes birds preen each other to show affection or trust. If your bird stops preening, it may be sick or depressed.

BITING

Young birds often peck their owner because they're at the stage where they explore everything with their beaks. But as a bird gets older, bites can be painful. Try not to scream because your pet will enjoy your reaction, just like biting a squeaky toy. Instead, put the bird down or back inside its cage and walk away. Once a bird understands that biting is not rewarded by your attention, it should stop.

FEATHER PLUCKING

Caged birds sometimes pluck out their feathers. Illness or parasites can be the cause, so if your pet is plucking its feathers, take it to the vet. Boredom, stress, or a poor diet can also be a cause for feather plucking, so give your bird attention, change its toys frequently, provide interesting foods, and make sure it isn't disturbed by other pets or noise. Loneliness can also be a problem, so if it won't stop, get your bird pal a companion!

NESTING

In spring, instinct tells birds to find a mate and produce young. Females may lay eggs even if they live alone and males might start collecting nest material. Nesting and sitting on eggs can make birds **territorial** and aggressive! If this happens, try reducing the amount of light your bird gets to less than 12 hours a day.

SIGNS OF AFFECTION

Wild birds feed their chicks (and show affection) by vomiting, or bringing up, food and dropping it into the other bird's mouth. Pet birds may bring up food onto their favorite human or toy. Don't be disgusted—it means they love you! Your bird may also preen your hair to show it cares.

TIME FOR BED

A good night's sleep is important for your pet's health. Wild birds go to sleep when it gets dark and wake up at dawn. If your birdcage is in a place where the light is on until late at night, cover it with a cloth or blanket and keep the noise down.

FEEDING YOUR FEATHERED FRIEND

Find out what your new pet has been eating before you bring it home, and stick to what it's used to while it settles in. If you want to change your bird's diet, do it slowly, adding new foods a little at a time.

FRESH TREATS

Fruits and vegetables are important for a bird's health. Leafy greens, carrots, peas, broccoli, beans, peppers, corn, and fruit are all good additions to your pet's diet. Always remove apple and pear seeds as they are poisonous to birds. Avoid avocado, onion, rhubarb, mushrooms, and too much spinach. Clear away leftovers daily.

A BASIC DIET

There are special seed mixtures you can buy to make sure your type of bird gets the **nutrients** it needs. Don't give your bird too much food at once. It will throw it about and pick out the seeds it likes best—usually the most fattening ones! Remove all uneaten food at the end of the day.

SET A GOOD EXAMPLE

Just like humans, birds can be suspicious of strange new foods. In the wild, they usually copy what other birds are eating, so if you want your bird to try something new, such as a piece of carrot or a blueberry, let it see you eating it first!

Cuttlebone is the internal shell of a cuttlefish. Putting one in your bird's cage is a good way to boost the calcium in its diet. Pecking and biting provides good exercise for your pet's jaws and helps keep its beak trim.

BIRD GRIT

Wild birds often swallow grit, or ground stone or sand, to help them grind up food. The grit goes to a muscly part of their stomach, called the gizzard, where it wears away seed husks so they can digest the seed inside. Most pet birds remove seeds from their husks before eating them, so they don't need grit. Only doves need grit because they swallow seeds whole.

CARING FOR YOUR PET

It's great to have fun with your bird buddy, but keeping a pet comes with responsibilities. These regular tasks will help to keep your feathered friend healthy and safe.

CAGE CLEANING

A dirty cage can lead to health problems for your bird (and it smells!) so be sure to keep your cage clean.

Every day
• change the floor liner
• clean food and water containers
• wipe down bars, perches, and toys

Every week
• wash the floor tray or grate
• soak and scrub the perches
• clean and change the toys

Every month
• scrub, rinse, and dry the whole cage

Top Tip! A second, smaller cage makes a safe temporary home for your pet and is useful for traveling to the vet.

NAIL TRIMMING

Pet birds need their nails trimmed regularly. Before you trim them, find a towel, nail clippers, paper towels, **styptic powder**, and a helper!

- Wrap the bird in the towel, speaking softly and gently to it.

- Ask your helper to gently hold the bird while you clip the sharp, pointed tip of the nail. If you cut too far down, the vein running through the claw will bleed. If this happens, wipe the blood off with a paper towel and dip the wound in styptic powder. Keep an eye on your bird afterward to make sure the bleeding has stopped.

- Give your bird a treat when you are done.

WING CLIPPING

Some bird owners clip their pet's wings, while others think it's unnatural and unkind. If done properly, trimming a bird's wing feathers doesn't stop it from flying but only slows it down. This may mean your pet gets into less mischief and can be allowed out of its cage more often. Also, clipping may save it from injuring itself in a crowded room. Clipping should never be done before a bird has fully learned to fly. If you decide that wing clipping is right for your bird, ask an expert or a vet to show you what to do. Similar to trimming nails, wing clipping doesn't hurt unless you cut down too far.

PLAYTIME

Let your bird out of its cage for a few hours each day so it can stretch its wings and explore. The exceptions are canaries and finches. These birds are less easy to tame and you may not be able to get them back into their cage. These birds need spacious homes.

HEALTH AND SAFETY

Birds are good at hiding signs of illness because they have many **predators** that would target a weak or sick bird. For this reason, it's important to get to know your bird's normal behavior so you can spot the signs that something is wrong before it's too late.

HOME HAZARDS

Birds are very sensitive to chemicals that are common in our homes. These include the fumes from nonstick pans, insect sprays, bleach, household cleaners, body sprays, nail polish, hair dye, scented candles, air fresheners, and all forms of smoke. In general, it's best to avoid all sprays around your bird.

PSITTACOSIS

Psittacosis is a very **contagious** disease that can be passed to other animals and humans. Symptoms include breathing difficulties, eye infections, and loose, watery droppings.

MITES

Mites dig into a bird's skin and feed on its blood. They are active at night, so watch out for your pet being restless then. Feather damage or crusts on your bird's legs or face are a sign of mites. Check at night with a flashlight and a magnifying glass for tiny black or red specks moving on your bird's head and feet. Buy anti-mite spray from a vet or pet store.

SIGNS OF ILLNESS

If your bird shows any of the symptoms below, you should take it to a vet.

- Sitting at the bottom of the cage with drooping wings, panting, and bobbing its tail
- Ruffled feathers that haven't been preened
- Red or runny nose or eyes
- A change in its droppings
- Difficulty breathing
- Weight loss

ULTRAVIOLET LIGHT

Just like humans, birds need ultraviolet light from sunshine to produce vitamin D. UV light cannot pass through glass, so birds that spend all their time indoors are lacking this essential vitamin. Bird experts think that installing a special UV bird lamp could cure many health issues, including feather plucking.

UNDERSTANDING YOUR BIRD

Birds can't always see each other, so sound is the best way for them to keep in touch. When they are closer together, birds also use body language to get their message across.

MAKING A NOISE

Wild birds use their voices to pass on information to others, such as checking in with other members of the flock when they're **foraging** or traveling, warning that there's a predator nearby, or chattering to let other birds know where they are settling down for the night. At dawn, male birds use the power of their songs to show off their health and strength, to attract mates, and to defend their territories. So, if you're looking for a bird that sings or talks, a male is best.

BIRD BODY LANGUAGE

If you understand your bird's actions, you can judge its mood and avoid a painful bite. Here are some common signs to look out for.

- **Freezing**
  A frightened bird may suddenly freeze. This is a defense against predators, who may not notice a motionless bird.

- **Stepping rapidly from side to side**
  This means a bird is excited. They often do this when they are pleased to see you!

- **Eye pinning**
  Parrots are able to make their **pupils** larger or smaller whenever they like. This means they are excited. But if they suddenly fluff up their feathers or fan out their tail too, they might be angry, so stay away!

CREST CLUES

If a cockatiel's crest, or the group of feathers on the top of its head, is held back with just the tip tilted up, it means the bird is happy and relaxed. If the crest is lifted, this means the bird is excited, but if the crest is held very high, it could mean your bird is scared. A flattened crest means the cockatiel is unhappy or, if it is crouching and hissing, it is feeling aggressive and should be left alone.

PET TALK

I can't reach the top of my head, so if I come toward you with my head bowed and stretched forward, please scratch me there.

- **Tail wagging or flipping**
  This is a sign of happiness, like a dog wagging its tail.

- **Beak grinding**
  Many birds grind their beaks as they drift off to sleep.

- **Head cocking**
  When a bird cocks its head, it is usually curious and wants to get a better view.

- **Growling or hissing**
  This is a clear warning that the bird wants to be left alone, especially if it's accompanied by eye pinning and raised neck feathers. When this happens, it's best to back off and give your bird buddy some space.

23

TAMING AND TRAINING

Give your bird at least two weeks to settle in before you start to handle it. Few canaries and finches enjoy being handled but they may step onto your finger if you have a good relationship. The first step is to get your bird used to your hand. Try holding it inside the cage with a treat on the palm to see if your pet will take it. Once your feathered friend associates your hand with a treat, you can teach it to "step up."

STEP UP

This is the first command a bird needs to learn. Open the door of the cage and put a treat on your palm, saying the words "step up" each time you do this. When your bird is used to coming to the door and taking the treat, place your hand in front of the door with the palm facing away from the cage. Hold the treat with your other hand, so your bird has to step onto the side of your index finger to get it. The next stage is to be able to move your hand with your bird standing on it.

STEP DOWN

This is the opposite of "step up," and you use it when returning your bird to its cage or perch. Place the hand holding the bird where you want your pet to go. Encourage your pet to step off, saying "step down." Give your bird a treat and a good head scratch when it does as you ask so it associates going back to its cage with something pleasant.

IMPORTANT

Every time you open the cage door, there's a chance that your bird might escape, so make sure the room is bird-proof first.

LEARNING TO TALK

Members of the parrot family, such as budgerigars, parrotlets, lovebirds, conures, and cockatiels, can learn to talk, but not all birds will. Some birds will whistle tunes or copy noises instead, such as a phone or doorbell ringing. Male birds are more likely to speak than females. Start by trying to teach your bird a few simple words such as its name or "hello," "bye-bye," or "goodnight." Even if a bird cannot speak, it will often understand what you're saying and obey simple commands.

PET TALK

Sometimes I'm busy doing something else, or just resting, so please leave me in peace if I don't do as you ask.

FUN AND GAMES

Most members of the parrot family are fun-loving creatures, and enjoy games such as fetch, peekaboo, and miniature bird basketball. Keeping them entertained when they're in their cage can be more difficult, so here are a few ideas.

FOODY FUN

Birds have to search for their food in the wild, so make some foraging toys to keep them occupied when they're in their cage. Cut the cardboard tube from a paper towel roll into pieces and hide some treats inside, then fold the ends over. If that's too easy for your pet to undo, tie some string around them (but don't use tape). Thread a selection of washed fruits and vegetables on a string and hang it from the top of the cage for your bird to peck. Include carrot, apple (with the seeds removed), broccoli, strawberry, radish, grapes, or pepper.

SUPER SHREDDERS

Members of the parrot family love to get their beaks into things and tear them to shreds! Hang some plain cardboard packaging or paper rolls in the cage. (It's best to avoid printed paper or card because inks contain chemicals). Make sure there are no staples, tape, or patches of glue that could harm your bird.

PET TALK

I like toys! But please don't give me a mirror. I'll think there's another bird in the cage and then I won't sing as much.

MAKE A SWING

Make a swing for your bird using a wooden hoop from a craft store. Use a leather lace, rope, or a chain to attach it to the top of the cage, and add a bell to the bottom for extra birdy fun.

NATURAL PERCHES

All birds enjoy some natural wood in their cage, either as perches or just to gnaw on, but many common woods are poisonous to pet birds. Here are some that are known to be safe: apple, ash, beech, crab apple, hazel, pear, and sycamore. Avoid any trees that may have been sprayed with chemicals. Wash the branches in a bird-safe disinfectant and rinse thoroughly. Ask an adult for asistance and bake the branches in a hot oven for about one hour to kill any bugs or insect eggs. Make sure the branches are cool before you put them in the cage.

HOME TIME

A cage should be a home for your pet, not a prison, so your bird pal should be happy to go back there after a few hours of freedom. Make sure your pet is hungry, then before it goes back, put some of its favorite food in the cage. It's useful to have a signal to tempt it back, too, such as tapping the cage or ringing a bell.

BIRD QUIZ

How much do you know about your feathered pal? Take this quiz to find out.

1 **What is a bird's cere?**

a. The area above its beak that includes its nostrils
b. An organ that grinds up food
c. A part of the tail

2 **Which birds like to live alone?**

a. Doves
b. Budgerigars
c. Canaries

3 **Which birds are most likely to talk?**

a. Females
b. Males
c. No difference

4 **Which of these birds lives longest?**

a. Finches
b. Conures
c. Doves

5 **Which of these foods is not suitable for birds?**

a. Avocado
b. Rhubarb
c. Both

6 **What is a good source of calcium for your bird?**

a. Cuttlefish bone
b. Carrot
c. Mushroom

7 **How often should you change the floor liner in your pet's cage?**

a. Every week
b. Every day
c. Every month

8 **What could be the cause if your bird is suddenly restless at night?**

a. It may have mites
b. It is bored
c. The room is too noisy

9 **What does it mean when a bird is eye pinning?**

a. Staring at its reflection in a mirror
b. Looking its owner straight in the eye
c. Making the pupils of the eyes larger and smaller

10 **What does it mean if a bird steps rapidly from side to side?**

a. It is frightened
b. It is excited
c. Its feet are painful

QUIZ ANSWERS

1 What is a bird's cere?

a. The area above its beak that includes its nostrils

2 Which birds like to live alone?

c. Canaries

3 Which birds are most likely to talk?

b. Males

4 Which of these birds lives longest?

b. Conures

5 Which of these foods is not suitable for birds?

c. Both

6 What is a good source of calcium for your bird?

a. Cuttlefish bone

7 How often should you change the floor liner in your pet's cage?

b. Every day

8 What could be the cause if your bird is suddenly restless at night?

a. It may have mites

9 What does it mean when a bird is eye pinning?

c. Making the pupils of the eyes larger and smaller

10 What does it mean if a bird steps rapidly from side to side?

b. It is excited

LEARNING MORE

BOOKS

Kalman, Bobbie and Kathryn Smithyman. *The Life Cycle of a Bird*. Crabtree Publishing, 2002.

MacAulay, Kelley and Bobbie Kalman. *Parakeets*. Crabtree Publishing, 2005.

Morgan, Sally. *Birds (Pets Plus)*. Smart Apple Media, 2012.

Titmus, Dawn. *Birds (Cool Pets for Kids)*. PowerKids Press, 2018.

WEBSITES

https://kids.nationalgeographic.com/animals/hubs/birds
This site offers games, images, videos, and tons of information about birds.

www.lovethatpet.com/small-pets/birds
This site is full of helpful information about bird care.

GLOSSARY

captivity To be confined in an area, not free to roam

contagious An illness that is easily spread

Cretaceous The period from 145 to 66 million years ago, when most dinosaurs were alive

descendant A relation of a person or animal that lived in the past

downy Soft, fluffy feathers that keep a bird warm

evolve To develop slowly or change over generations

foraging Searching for food

fossil The remains of an animal or plant that lived long ago

hollow Empty inside

instinct A natural pattern of behavior

mite A tiny bug related to a spider

nutrients The substances in food that help living things grow and stay healthy

parasite An animal that lives in or on another creature and feeds from it, often by sucking its blood

predator An animal that hunts other creatures

preen To clean and straighten feathers

pupil The black part of the eye

reflect To throw back light or sound

roost Settle down to sleep

species A group of closely related organisms

styptic powder A powder that stops bleeding by sealing the injured vein

tame To train a living thing to be friendly and gentle

territorial The way a bird behaves when it is defending its nesting site

ultraviolet (UV) The part of sunlight that is invisible to humans but visible to birds

INDEX